AF432138

THE GOD OF THE COVENANT

Our collection

Christian Notebook Collection

The GOD of the Covenant

Translated version of "Le DIEU de l'Alliance"

2016

Mimyelle GNIGOU KASSI

KOEUR de Miel Editions

ISBN: 979-10-96052-12-7

Mimyelle GNIGOU KASSI

KOEUR de Miel Editions

6 Rue d'Armaillé, 75017 Paris

Legal deposit: September 2020.

I pray to Thee, O Lord, JEHOVAH Father, The Most kind, Thou GOD of the Covenant. May You use this book, to bring to all the people who will read it, the Wisdom and Peace necessary for the stability of their homes.

All the Glory be unto to Thee, in JESUS name!

Thank you, dear husband Thierry KASSI, for your support throughout the writing of this book. Be blessed in all respects, vase of honor in the hands of Christ!

I dedicate this work to all the brave and virtuous women and to the twins of May 20th.
May you be blessed, for continuing to be a blessing to this world!

Foreword

Our GOD is the GOD of the Covenant. He instituted Marriage and the Bible declares that everything He does is perfect.

Nevertheless today, many couples are experiencing and living a situation of want. While everything started out well, the wine is running out, the flavor is leaving the house and things seem to be going sour. This is unfortunately the same regardless of the races of the people involved, their cultures and even their religions!

'From the beginning it was not so' Cf. Mat 19:8. 'An enemy has done this'. Cf. Mat 13:28. The devil is out to destroy marriages, even to the point of attacking their foundations. Cf. Jn 10:10

However, the first miracle of JESUS revealed in the Bible was performed during a wedding at Cana, when the couple needed wine. Cf. **John 2.** This is indeed the sign that GOD wants to save all troubled homes.

This book does not pretend to identify all the possible reasons for the failures and difficulties encountered by couples. Its purpose is to share with you what the Word of GOD says about the Covenant, especially the Covenant of Marriage, and how willing JESUS is, to come to the rescue of households in distress. The goal therefore is to renew our thinking, by calibrating it on what the Word of GOD, the compass that leads to the happiness of mankind, says.

This book will focus on the woman, covering the two-winged aspects of her life: her GOD given Mission- her potentialities-

as well as her personality as a wife, mother or simply as a woman. Certainly, the success of a marriage involves both husband and wife. However, we will voluntarily choose to focus mainly on the wife's contribution, as if everything depended solely on her, and the GOD of victories will step in and crown her efforts.

The Word of GOD says*: "The wise woman builds her house, and the foolish woman overthrows it with her own hands.* **"Proverbs 14:1** This passage implies that the Lord has given women the power to ensure the stability and durability of their homes. It is therefore our responsibility as women to find out how to go about it, by choosing the right weapons the Lord has placed in our hands to achieve it.

Although the focus is the covenant in marriage, this book will be an extremely useful tool for those who are not yet married and are waiting for this bliss. It will help them prepare for their future homes, carved after the pattern of the Word of GOD.

In addition, this book will enable men to realize that women are a treasure that the Lord entrusts to them.

May the Holy Spirit through the pages of this book, teach and guide the heart of every reader. Amen.

Chapitre I.   HAPPINESS IN MARRIAGE

A.   Happiness in marriage according to the world

I. <u>"They lived happily ever after and had many children."</u>

That, in a nutshell, is the definition of marriage the world serves us. We often imagine that after marriage, our lives will turn to be a fairy tale caroused by a love that overcomes all difficulties and resists all external temptations. We anticipate waking up every morning beside someone who will make us forget all the worries of this world by loving us more than anything else, with a love we have always dreamt of: to be the center of our partner's life and together spending each day like a long, calm river, where love is the master.

This fictional vision of love is sown in the minds of children from an early age by cartoons, and is later on nurtured by soap operas, novels and rosewater musical compositions.

Besides, a "true man in love" is immediately recognizable: he very often, offers gifts to his wife; invites her to a restaurant or somewhere else. He often reassures her by saying "I love you". Many women may be beautiful, but he only has eyes for his chosen one. He is attentive, gallant; always opening to her the door; offers to come and do the shopping; carries her belongings; takes care of all the house expenses. He never contradicts her and can listen to her talk for hours without getting tired. Ideally, he thinks one day, of declaring his love in a spectacular way, "like in the movies". So right there, that is the jackpot!

The expectations in marriage are therefore based on this vision, and even if before the wedding, the groom was not quite what was hoped for, somewhere in her heart, consciously or unconsciously, the girl expects the wedding to unveil the Prince Charming within. Besides, is not the fact of getting married, especially in great pomp, the beginning of this revelation since the 'hero' has passed the stage of declaring his flame before everyone? Unfortunately, many brides are disappointed only a short time after their wedding, because they do not see their man turn into that prince charming. The very one who, sometimes before, said he loved them and even married them!

Are we really tailoring our ideals after the thoughts of God by reasoning the way we do? Hoping for a perfect marriage is not bad, quite the contrary. However, the definition of the term "PERFECT MARRIAGE" needs to be reviewed in order to avoid disappointment and discouragement. Some difficulties may arise, for example misunderstanding or financial constrains but true Love-*GOD KIND OF LOVE*-overcomes everything Cf. 1Corinthians 13:4. Only the Marriage before GOD, in the church guarantees God's blessing which in return will undoubtedly forbid any problem from disturbing unjustifiably the future home.

II. <u>The "realistic" theories</u>

On the other hand, there are people who see things differently. They claim to be more "realistic". In fact, they do not expect their man to be perfect or even caring. These are usually people who have been either hurt by catastrophic marriage examples they may have witnessed at a young age, or even by pre-marital relationships that ended badly. These people end up saying to themselves that there is no such thing as a happy marriage. They put up with the situation, because as partners, they always end up disappointed. Consequently, such persons come into the marriage on the defensive, and are constantly waiting for that 'fatal day' when the next disappointment will knock at their household door. They are convinced that what has happened to others will certainly happen to them! Know this clearly: no one can build something lasting, on a defeatist foundation ...

III. <u>The experience of others</u>

We often hear people say: "We don't get marry to be happy, but to make the counterpart happy".

This assertion, true only in part, puts us on a slippery slope. It is true in the sense that out of love, we first concern ourselves with the happiness of the spouse. Such a one-sided belief which relegates our personal fulfillment in second position, is false. We marry precisely because two are better than one! Cf. Ecclesiastes 4:9

Secondly, this assertion puts each partner in the legitimate expectation that the other will do everything to make him or her happy. In this case as well, the other becomes the source of our happiness. The questions are: does this 'source' have the capacity to water us indefinitely? Can it not dry up? Do we have the right source, when we know that Man in nature is selfish and limited? There is, therefore, a problem of reliability of source!

Generally, conceptions and expectations in marriage are based on advice and guidance received from predecessors; currents of thought and other assertions usually based on their own experiences.
Some people even go so far as to evaluate the possible period of happiness in a marriage. For example, a person I consider to be a 'big sister' once told me: "the first 2 years of marriage are the best". This assumes that for the additional years, nothing is guaranteed.

Knowing that we marry for life, it is a little shocking to hear such a thing. What then should one expect the rest of such a fragile married life to be?

It becomes a big disappointment when misunderstandings arise as soon as you enter the marriage. 'It hasn't been 2 years yet!' you remark in disillusion, implying: without a doubt, the 2 years happiness verdict is not enough provision, if those 2 most beautiful years of your married life are being wasted! What will happen afterwards?

The more optimistic ones say, "if you made it through the first 7 years, then your marriage will STAND". The reasoning is simple: after 7 years, you know the other person well enough, to discern how to react, how to handle adversities etc. This thought is inaccurate because, first, it assumes the spouse character will not be subject to changes. It does. People do change and adopt behaviors they did not have 7 years earlier depending on the circumstances at hand. Secondly, on one hand, it appears as if we give 7 years of expected marital trials and difficulties to manifest themselves. The set limit beyond which they can no longer spread their threatening tentacles, at least to some extent. On the other hand, after 7 years, temptation is believed to have no longer effect on the couple. In short, according to this school of thought, after seven 7 years, the dream life can begin. Maybe that is because it is generally accepted that the number 7 is the number of Perfection.

You will agree with me that, based on the analysis of this stand, it is completely erroneous to attribute the strength of a couple to a specific number of years. Some self-appointed marriage counselors do not hesitate to advise the fiancés to live together for a certain number of years, in order to get to know each other better and ideally anticipate the 7 years. Thus, once married, there will not be much time left for frailty in the household. It is a trap. Many couples have thus become bogged down in pre-marital cohabiting and can no longer get out of its thorn. Such moves are proving that we do not realize that the obstacles to happiness in marriage are orchestrated by the devil's maneuvers and that he is not limited by time estimates, but rather, hindered by the means of prayer. The irrefutable proof is the plethoric number of divorces after the famous 7 years.

In either position, the major mistake is to base happiness in marriage on the counterpart's ability to make his or her partner happy!

The Bible says: *"Better to turn to the Lord than to rely on a man!* **"Psalms 118:8.**

We do not have the pretense to says that man is not able to make his fellow happy, but it is in GOD that the blessing is full and perennial. **Proverbs 10:22** indisputably settles the issue; "*It is the blessing of the LORD that maketh rich, and he maketh it not sorrowful*".

It is GOD who created us, and as our Manufacturer, HE knows what we need to be happy in the T-tempo.

IV. <u>Refer to the manufacturer's instructions!</u>

The great disappointment comes from there: the distorted basis of marriage. We are basing our expectations on principles that are far from being verified, instead of relying on the Author of the institution called marriage.

Buying a product and expecting it to do things it is not intended to, lead to frustration. For intense, if you buy a microwave oven, and you expect it to be a vacuum cleaner too, because you want to make your life at home much easier, you'll be disappointed that it can't vacuum. No matter how much you grumble, as long as you do not refer to the user manual or the manufacturer of the machine to have a clear understanding of the appliance purpose, its functions and attributes, you will not be able to enjoy it fully. Of course, nothing prevents you from imagining a lot of functions the device could be used for, but when you get to use it, reality will always catch up with you: you will not benefit from its full potential and instead of making your life more comfortable, it will bring you frustration, disappointment and anger.

Likewise, if you and I do not turn to the Author of the institution of marriage, who is GOD, and to His notice which is His Word, we will always be frustrated. We may choose to invent attributes and purposes for marriage, but if that is not what the Lord has established, then, we will unfailingly be disappointed.

On the contrary, when we start from what the Lord has said or established, we avoid many frustrations and experience the happiness that comes from Him. This does not exclude trials, but we know that we can count on our GOD to lead us out of difficulties, because we are in His will.

Thus, should we turn to the Lord, to seek what is His will, the objectives and reasons why He created marriage and what are in His mind, the characteristics of a happy marriage?

From this point on, it is legitimate as His offspring, to base our expectations on what GOD has promised us in His Word, and to hope for His help when difficulties arise.

Ephesians 5:17 "Therefore do *not be foolish but understand what the Lord's will is*.

B.   Happiness in marriage according to the Word of GOD

The Apostle Paul admonishes us to be renewed in our intelligence, in the way we see and understand things. **Romans 12:2 *"Do not be conformed to this world, but be transformed by the renewal of your minds, that you may discern what is the good, acceptable and perfect will of God"*.**

Unlike the unbeliever, the Christian must not think, act and speak according to the standard of the world. His reference should be the Word of GOD, which is the light on his path; the lamp on his feet, and the indispensable compass that guides him on the path of his destiny, so as to live a blessed and fulfilled life.

Psalms 119:105 *"Your word is a lamp to my feet, And a light* **to** *my path.*

I pray that our inner being may be renewed according to the revelation of the Word of GOD.

I. <u>GOD: The source of true human happiness</u>

Since the dawn of time, Man has been searching for happiness and each step he takes, in the attempt to make him advance towards this ideal, seems to be inadequate. It is often said that he is "eternally unsatisfied".

For example, the conscientious college student has the impression that having his Brevet and entering high school will bring indescribable happiness to his life. This is the goal he sets for himself and hopes to have a certain level of satisfaction once this goal is achieved. Finally, as soon as he enters high school, he realizes that it is rather the Baccalaureate that he needs; then the entrance exam to the engineering class; then work; then marriage; then achievements etc....

A lot of people misunderstand happiness to be measured in terms of possessions and intellectual achievements, misconception that unfortunately, birthed the high percentage of cases of depressions and suicides among the rich and famous of this world.

If happiness is not measured by the accumulation of material goods - which certainly contribute to it – It is therefore striking to notice that man's quest seems never to stop despite the gain of satisfaction eluding his heart.

Yet the Bible validates the possibility of attaining the peak of happiness in all facets of life.

Job 22:21 "*Hold fast to God, and you will have peace, and you will enjoy happiness.*

Isaiah 48:18 "*Oh that you would heed my commandments! Your welfare would be like a river, and your happiness like the waves of the sea*".

Jeremiah 32:39 "*I will give them one heart and one way, that they may fear me always, for their good and for the good of their children after them.*

Man's happiness is only found in GOD and in the observance of His laws. GOD, who created man, knows exactly what man needs for his development at every stage of his life. Our GOD is a loving Father who strives to give His children what they need, even if sometimes it may seem contrary to our expectations. As an illustration, a child whose parents send to school to sit under tutors, is not necessarily happy about it etc., but the parents themselves know that it is for the good of their little one, so they do not take into account the child's recriminations. Another example is that of parents who have their children fitted with braces. They are aware of the pain and discomfort the braces bring to the child, but in the interest of his future well-being, its appliance is still maintained.

If we are convinced that our parents, who did not create us but gave birth to us; who cannot be everywhere with us; who cannot endure our sufferings in our place love us. How much more should we be convinced of the love of GOD Who created us, who stays with us all our life and ultimately did not hesitate to give His only begotten Son, to die in our stead, for the salvation of our souls!

In **Matthew 6:25-34** the Lord JESUS gives a very clear teaching on this subject: "*Therefore I say to you, Do not be anxious about the food and drink you need to live, or about the clothing you need for your body. Life is more important than food and the body is more important than clothing, right?*

26 Look at the birds. They neither sow nor reap, neither do they gather crops into barns, but your Father who is in heaven feeds them. Aren't you worth much more than the birds?

27 Which of you can prolong his life a little by the care he takes for himself?

28 And why do you worry about clothing? Observe how the flowers of the field grow: they do not work; they do not make themselves clothing.

29 Yet I tell you, not even Solomon, with all his wealth, had clothes as beautiful as one of these flowers.

30 God so clothes the grass of the field, which is there today, and tomorrow will be thrown into the fire: then will he not much more clothe you yourselves? How weak is your trust in him!

31 Don`t be anxious, therefore, saying, "What are we to eat? What are we to drink? What are we to put on?"

32 It is the Gentiles who seek all these things continually. But your Father in heaven knows that you need them.

<u>33 Be interested first with all that concern the Kingdom of God and the righteous life He is asking for, and God will grant you all the rest also.</u>

34 Do not therefore worry about tomorrow, for tomorrow will worry about itself. Each day has its sorrow. »

We must trust in GOD's love and believe in His goodness and faithfulness to take care of us.

Every time we try to find happiness in something or someone else than GOD, our soul deep inside remains thirsty and unsatisfied.

It is by seeking the Lord with a sincere and whole heart that we achieve happiness.

Deuteronomy 30:9-10: "*The LORD your God will make you happy by making all the work of your hands, your children, the flocks of your herds, and the produce of your soil flourish. Indeed, the Lord will again take pleasure in your happiness, just as He took pleasure in that of your ancestors,*

When you obey the LORD your God, keeping his commandments and his statutes written in this book of the law, when you return to the LORD your God with all your heart and with all your soul".

No wonder, the first divinely intentional 4 words of the Bible are: *"In the beginning, GOD*. Genesis 1:1.

II. <u>The woman, a true treasure for her husband and for humanity...</u>

There is a close link between marriage, the creation of woman, and the happiness of man. Indeed, originally, GOD created woman in order to fill a void, remedying the limit in man. **Genesis 2:18**: "And *the LORD GOD said, it is not good for man to be alone; I will make him a helper like unto him.* "».

The woman is a precious added value, a treasure for her husband.

1. <u>Woman is a gift from the Lord for the happiness of man...</u>

Proverbs 18:22: "*He that finds a wife finds happiness; it is a blessing from the Lord.*

Proverbs 31:12 "*She never does him harm, but she gives him happiness all the days of his life*".

Proverbs 19:14 says clearly: "A *house and riches may be inherited from parents, but a prudent wife is a gift from the Lord*".

This means that the woman who tries to conform to the Lord's recommendations is a real treasure for her family. In fact, a wise woman is the reward that JEHOVAH gives to those who are faithful to Him. It is like the crown that honors an overcomer.

Proverbs 12:4 "*A righteous woman is her husband's crown, but she who causes shame is like the decay in her bones*.

Psalms 128:3-4 "*Your wife is like a fruitful vine in your house; your sons are like olive plants around your table. Blessed is the man who fears the Lord*.

2. <u>The woman, support for the ministry</u>

The Bible mentions in the Old Testament, as in the New, several women who were a real support to GOD Servants.

Support can be ministered to at different levels:

a. <u>*Hospitality and service :*</u>

1 Kings 17:9 "*Arise, go to Zarephath, which belongs to Sidon, and dwell there. Behold, there I have commanded a widowed woman to feed you*".

2 Kings 4:8-10 "*One day Elisha passed through Sunem. There was a distinguished woman there, who urged him to take food. And whenever he passed by, he went to her house to eat.* »

Luke 10:38 *"While Jesus was on the way with his disciples, he entered a village, and a woman named Martha received him into her house.*

Acts 16:14-15 *"One of them was called Lydia. [...]. After being baptized with her family, she invited us, saying, "If you judge me faithful to the Lord, come into my house and stay there," and she strongly urged us to accept.*

b. *Moral and Financial support*

Matthew 27:55 *"There were many women there watching from afar; they had accompanied Jesus from Galilee to serve him.*

Luke 23:27 *"He was followed by a great crowd of people and women who beat their breasts and lamented him.*

Luke 8:3 *"Joanna, wife of Chuza, Herod's steward, Susanna, and many others, who were assisting him with their goods.*

Proverbs 31:26 *"She speaks wisely, she knows how to give advice with kindness".*

3. Woman reveals JESUS to the world

Before the wedding at Cana, no one had seen the Lord JESUS perform a miracle. Nobody had received the revelation of His divine nature, powerful to come to the rescue from man's worries and misery. Mary had that revelation of Who JESUS was, since the day of the Annunciation by angel Gabriel. She would therefore instigate His unveiling to the servants at the wedding, unveiling that will mark the beginning of His Mission to mankind at large.

John 2:3-5 "When *the wine ran out, Jesus' mother said to him, 'They have no more wine. Jesus answered her, "What do you want with me, woman? My hour has not yet come". His mother said to the servants, "Do whatever he tells you. ""* »

Finally, JESUS performed the miracle of turning water into wine, and the marriage was blessed. The Bible says in **verse 11:** "*This was the first of the miraculous signs which Jesus did at Cana of Galilee. He manifested his glory, and his disciples believed in him.*

Likewise, the Samaritan village in **John 4** had never heard of JESUS, until the Samaritan woman proclaimed Him**.**

John 4:19 "*Many of the Samaritans in that city believed in Jesus because of the words of the woman who testified, 'He told me all that I have done.'"* ».

On the morning of the Resurrection, women were the first to receive and announce the Good News of Christ's Resurrection.

Revealing Christ to the world is a duty for us women!

4. The woman is a wedding ring

Galatians 4:24 "*These things are allegorical; for these women are two covenants. ....* »

The fact that woman is likened to a covenant leads us to consider the word "covenant" and ultimately, GOD as "The GOD of the Covenant".

Chapitre II. The GOD of the Covenant!

Throughout the history of Israel, our GOD introduces Himself as the GOD of the Covenant. The word "Covenant" appears several times in the Bible. Then what does it really mean and what does the covenant our Lord makes with us, change for us?

The alliance is a union, an agreement, a pact sealed between 2 parties. **It is a reciprocal commitment, between the two parties, which unites their destinies.** A country that makes an alliance with another, commits itself to help the latter in case of external attack, thus exposing its military, logistic, strategic, financial resources..., for a battle stakes it was not concern with. This is the reason why, in politics, deciding to form an alliance with someone is a strategic choice that is made after careful calculations and in-depth reflection, because those stakes are serious and involve the entire political future of the parties.

This agreement translates into a set of rules and principles to which the parties adhere, with the aim of achieving a certain good. In general, the terms of this alliance are recorded and materialized, so that each party remembers its commitments. For example, we speak of alliance treaties between two regional powers.

In Africa, particularly in Côte d'Ivoire, there are alliances between certain tribes and/or families. When 2 families seal an alliance, it is not uncommon to see an endangered member of the allied families, involved in a confrontation, being defended and rescued by his counterpart, before even the latter trying to understand neither what is happening nor who is right or wrong.

Marriage is by far the most important alliance, the most engaging and therefore the strongest. Man and woman give and commit themselves to each other <u>for life</u>. The Bible itself goes further by saying that *"they become one flesh"*. This is no longer a simple sharing of lots, but a complete fusion. The covenant is recorded in a register and the family book. It is materialized by a ring called "Alliance " which is constantly worn, making the commitment visible to all. The parties become allied families, for beyond the simple document of a marriage certificate, they find themselves bound by blood. We speak therefore of the "sacred bonds of marriage".

A.   The Wedding Ring

I. <u>Characteristics of the alliance :</u>

- ✓ The woman joins voluntarily. She is willing, otherwise it is no longer an alliance.
- ✓ It is beneficial for both parties.
- ✓ It commits each of the parties to the other according to a written agreement.

The Covenant in the Bible is a covenant between GOD and mankind, made with the patriarchs Noah, Abraham, Jacob-Israel, then extended to their descendants, Israel and finally, with the coming of Christ, to all men.

This Covenant keeps the same permanent characteristics throughout the Bible:

- ➤ **It is concluded on the initiative of GOD** who asks men to believe in Him and commits Himself to defend them, provide for their needs, and ensure their happiness.
- ➤ **It is eternal** like GOD Himself.
- ➤ **It commits Man to respect the precepts GOD commands him; and instructions** contained in the Bible.
- ➤ **It is materialized** by visible and invisible things among which the rainbow, the tables of the law; the Ark of the Covenant; the Word of GOD; the Blood the Lamb…

In Genesis 9: 12-13 for instance, *God said: " This is the sign of the covenant which I have made between me and you and every living creature that is with you for all generations: I have set **my bow** among the clouds, and it shall be for a sign of the covenant between me and the earth".*

The covenant is often equated with marriage. JEHOVAH presents Himself as a loving spouse.

Isaiah 62:4 *"You shall no longer be called forsaken, neither shall your land be called desolate; but you shall be called my pleasure in it, and your land shall be called wife; for the LORD has pleasure in you, and your land shall have a husband. »*

Ephesians 5:25 *"Husbands, love your wives as Christ loved the church. He gave Himself for her. »*

This means that the Covenant the Lord establishes with his children is a covenant which undenied commitment is at the height of its expression.

Isaiah 50:1 *"Thus says the Lord: 'Where is the letter of divorce by which I put away your mother? "'' »*

Throughout the Bible, the Lord never ceases to commit Himself to His children and to anyone who believes in Him and His promises. If man has faith in GOD and keeps His commandments, he is rewarded because GOD will commit Himself to him during his life and grants him eternity after death.

II. <u>The GOD of the Covenant of Marriage</u>

After creating Eve as man's helpmate, GOD gives her to Adam. In **Genesis 3:12**, the man answered and said, "This *is the woman whom YOU gave me to be my companion...*"; This was the very first marriage, orchestrated by GOD Himself!

Marriage is therefore the answer to man's loneliness, suffering and fatigue, and woman, the expression of this provision. 1 Corinthians 11:9 "*And the man was not created for the woman's sake, but the woman for the man's sake.*

From this verse, the woman can already understand her first mission as a wife.

Notice that HE made a woman and not a second man. **Mark 10:6** "*But in the beginning of creation, God made man and woman.*

Yet the Lord does not stop there. He does not just create the woman and lay her down beside Adam in the Garden of Eden. He has a greater and more complex plan.

Further on, it is written: "*Therefore shall a man leave his father and mother, and shall cleave to his wife, and they shall become <u>one flesh</u>*" **Genesis 2:24.**

This passage is repeated several times in the Gospel, notably in **Mark 10:8-9**.

It is a real mystery! Hence for GOD, after marriage, there are no longer 2 people but only one.

I would like to make at this point, a needful clarification about divorce: In the Gospel of Matthew, the Lord states categorically that there is no room for divorce in marriage. Although the disciples react to this new teaching, the answer of JESUS is an unapologetic disclosure:

Matthew 19:10-12: *His disciples said to him, "If this is the condition of a man towards a woman, it is better not to marry.*

He answered them: "Not all understand this word, but only those to whom it is given.

Indeed, there are eunuchs who have been eunuchs from their mother's womb, others have been made eunuchs by men, and there are some who have made themselves eunuchs for the sake of the kingdom of heaven. He who can understand, let him understand.

In other words, marriage is not for everyone. Some have the possibility of fulfilling their life mission without going through the sacred union of marriage. Only those to whom it is given. "That" here is put for 'marriage'. Jesus goes on to say that some, naturally, are eunuchs from their mother's womb, while others become eunuchs to serve GOD.

According to the Larousse dictionary, an eunuch is a castrated man charged with important administrative and military functions, as well as guarding the imperial harems. This is also the name given to officers of the Jewish kings, who oversaw guarding the chamber, although they were not mutilated. Thus, the eunuchs are not necessarily castrated, or powerless. Some of them impose themselves to live with their sexual urge under control, for the sake of the Kingdom of GOD.

What does that mean?

Marriage was certainly created and instituted by GOD, for the well-being of Man, but it is not an obligation, nor a fashion phenomenon. Not everyone is necessarily called to marry. Based on JESUS assertion: "those to whom it is given", someone can choose to live as a eunuch for the benefit of GOD's work, provided of course, he respects his commitment. The Apostle Paul suggests to the Corinthians who can, to choose celibacy in order to focus on the work of GOD. However, he balances the scales by saying that it is better to marry than to burn with desire. In short, let those who cannot make this sacrifice marry!

1 Corinthians 7:1 "...*it is good for a man not to take a wife. However, to avoid sexual immorality, let every man have his wife and every woman have her husband.*

If then celibacy can be a choice of life, this confirms that marriage is neither, as some people seem to believe, the ultimate blessing for a woman, nor the only source of her happiness and fulfillment! In the same light, celibacy is not a mark of bad behavior, nor a handicap otherwise, it would be very unfair of GOD to offer it as an option!

In any case, there is a probability of loneliness to be feared, because there is no guarantee that after a marriage, one could be exempted from becoming a widow immediately. However, we have the assurance that GOD does not abandon His children to solitude because according to the Psalmist, *God gives a family to those who were forsaken.* **(Psalms 68:6-7)**.

Here is one more proof that the blessing, the true happiness of Man is experienced only when he is in perfect communion with GOD, Who has the capability to take care of Men needs in all respects.

Woman, your worth does not depend on marriage or a relationship with a man. Just as the value of a garment is determined by its designer, so your value is defined by your Creator!

You were desired and created by the Most High GOD, Who made the heaven, earth, and shaped the universe! You are exactly the one GOD wants. Despite your weaknesses and limits that dimmed the spark of your strength and abilities, you are the fruit of His reflection and love. Do not despise yourself!

"You made me what I am, and you wove me in my mother's womb. Thank you for making me such a wonderful creature" **Psalm 139:13-14**.

Before entering marriage, it is advisable to discern your vocation beforehand, in order to know if you are really called to marriage. There are marriage preparation courses in the churches for this purpose. One does not marry to do as one's girlfriends do, nor to be honored on a given day. Marriage is a true calling; a ministry; a vocation. When one commits oneself to it, it must be done with seriousness and determination, for like in any other mission, we will be called before GOD to account for the manner we have carried out that assignment.

III. <u>Tripartite Union for Life</u>

"Let no man put asunder what God hath joined together."
Mark 10:9

This warning will be repeated by JESUS in the Gospels several times.

The Lord's position on divorce is therefore clearly stated. Those who were thinking of going down this road, consider again the contraindication, the ruling of the Lord.

At this point I would like to stop and speak to everyone who is suffering from a divorce that has already been granted. May the Lord heal you from that wound and may He bind your broken hearts!

Indeed, no matter what one may let it seem, there is no honest person who gets married with the aim of getting divorced. Divorce always creates a feeling of great distress often, with the rest of life, deeply marked by regret, guilt or anger.

I repeat, I pray that the Lord will heal you and bind your broken hearts.

GOD does not blame His children. He is always ready to welcome us, to restore us and to make us forget the sufferings of the past, if we come to Him with a pure and sincere heart.

I also want to tell you that even if you think that there is nothing more to do because everything is over, and above all, even if you don't want to hear anything about your

spouse anymore; As long as you got married in the church, before GOD, He is able to change your hearts, revive love, and restore that wrecked marriage!

He is the One who restores the years that the devourer has stolen. Trust in GOD!

On the other hand, if for one of these reasons: the case of a remarried spouse or a situation of extreme danger, a return to marriage is impossible or needs to be avoided, it is necessary to know how to turn the page and move on.

Some women develop health issues as a result of their marriage breakdown. They consider their lives wasted and their ministry nipped in the bud because of the lifelong and indelible stain of divorce.

GOD is the One who determines the purpose of our life. He knows your past yet, still calls you to serve Him. Very often, what may look like failure, is used by GOD for His Glory.

I would like to encourage you to get your head up and get out of the guilt. Your calling is not a reflection of the state of your marriage. GOD does not call perfect or capable people, but He makes capable those He calls.

If GOD can use for His work, people who have not excelled in studies for example, He can also use people who seem to have failed emotionally. Your experience will certainly help other couples who are going through what you have already gone through.

Very often, the situations that look like bitter failures to Men are the very ones the Lord uses for His Glory:

- JESUS came to proclaim salvation and deliverance for all men. He even saved a criminal while on the cross but died the worst of death. As a result, He became an object of mockery because it seemed absurd!
Matthew 27:42 *"He has saved others, but he cannot save himself! If he is king of Israel, let him come down from the cross, and we will believe in him.*

- The Samaritan woman whose sentimental life seemed catastrophic (for she was at her 5th man, without ever having been married) is indeed the one the Lord used, to reveal Himself to her whole village.
"Many of the Samaritans in that city believed in Jesus because of the words of the woman who gave this testimony: "He told me everything I have done. **John 4:39**

Let nothing and no one prevent you from doing what the Lord puts in your heart, for His work!

And GOD will restore you in a way you cannot imagine.

B. Application of the Covenant with GOD in Marriage

I. Interests of a tripartite alliance

We know that GOD is the creator of heaven and earth, of the visible and invisible universe. We know as well that in Him there is no shadow of variation and that His faithfulness lasts forever.

James 1:17 *"Every excellent grace and every perfect gift comes down from above, from the Father of lights, in whom there is no change or shadow of variation.*

We also know that He is the Ancient of days and that He is JEHOVAH. He holds the hearts of men in His hands and is omniscient (He knows everything), omnipotent (He can do everything) and omnipresent (He is everywhere at the same time).

Getting married in the church automatically guarantees having such a GOD as ally, and this changes everything in our life. It changes everything: we are no more ignorant; we anticipate the future; no longer fear anyone or anything, because we have the Almighty GOD who **sworn an oath to be on** our side. How wonderful that is!!!!

Everyone recognizes the radiance of the children of Israel. They excel in everything they do or touch, regardless of the field.

Writer Mark Twain said in the 19th century about the children of Israel: *"[The children of Israel] are curiously and conspicuously the intellectual aristocracy ... The contributions to the list of great names in literature, science, the arts, music, finance and medicine are beyond measure ...".*

These extraordinary achievements are simply due to their deep commitment to the Alliance with GOD and the resulting promises of excellence.

Deuteronomy 28:3 *"The LORD will make you the head and not the tail, you will always be on top and never be below, when you obey the commandments of the LORD your God, which I command you this day, when you keep them and do them.*

Considering the above, what would be the impact on our lives as children of GOD if we took to heart, to believe and respect our relationship with GOD by putting Him above anything else? We are the heirs of a Covenant greater than the first one established in the Old Testament, because our covenant was concluded at the price of the Blood of JESUS CHRIST, true GOD and true Man.

1 Corinthians 6:20 *"For you have been redeemed at a great price. Therefore, give glory to God in your body [and in your spirit which belong to God].*

The fact of committing ourselves to the Covenant that GOD Himself has established in advance guarantees us His backing and His faithfulness throughout our life, because GOD never abandons His children. This saves us many worries and struggles!

I like very much this example of GOD's faithfulness in Abraham's marriage.

Let us read together **Genesis 20:3-6** *"Then GOD appeared to Abimelech in a dream in the night, and said to him: Thou shalt* *die for the woman whom thou hast taken away, because she is married. And Abimelech, who had not yet come near to her, answered and said: Lord, wilt thou destroy even a righteous nation? Did he not tell me that she was his sister, and she herself did not say that he was her brother? With a true heart and innocent hands, I have acted".*

GOD said to him in his dream: "I also know that thou hast acted with an upright heart, so that I myself have kept thee from sinning against me. That is why I did not allow you to touch her. Now return this man's wife, for he is a prophet. He will pray for you and you will live. But if you do not give her back, know that you will die, you and all that belongs to you.

Both Abraham and his wife schemed and lied. Consequently, the king did not know Sarah was married. 2 mitigating circumstances that could have prevented the Lord from acting in favor of their marriage, but no! The Lord in His move to solve the situation not only presents Himself personally to Abimelech and threatens him with a death sentence, but also shows His supremacy over the enfolding of the event! How astonishing that is: GOD affirms being the One who withheld Abimelech from touching Sara!!! Abraham did not need to take any action against the king to get his wife back.

GOD can stop other women from getting their hands on your husband!

Same scenario with Mary, mother of JESUS, whose future marriage was dangerously threatened by the pregnancy of Christ she was carrying. Mary did not need to try to convince Joseph, her fiancé, not to abandon her. The Lord took care of it on her behalf, in a dream. Yes, they were only engaged at the time, but

GOD was already interested in that union, probably because the fiancés had tried to commit it to Him.

Matthew 1:19-20 "*Joseph, her fiancé, was an upright man and did not want to denounce her publicly; he decided to secretly break off his engagement. As he was thinking about it, an angel of the Lord appeared to him in a dream and said, "Joseph, a descendant of David, do not be afraid to marry Mary, for by the action of the Holy Spirit she is expecting a child.* »

I am telling you again, sister/daughter, go and rest. If you got married in the church before GOD and you are faithful to your covenant (with GOD and with your husband), you do not need to get bogged down in useless palaver. Remain serene and rest. Your GOD will take care of restoring your couple. In your rest, lays the peace of your home, and as a bonus, GOD will force your enemies to give you allegiance and honor. Your GOD fights for you!

Genesis 20:14-15 "And *Abimelech took sheep and oxen, and menservants and maidservants, and gave them to Abraham. And he gave Sarah his wife back to him, saying, "My land is before you. Settle down where it pleases you*" ".

II. <u>Praying on the basis of the Alliance</u>

The Lord commits Himself based on His Word.

If you are in a covenant with Him in your marriage, you can validly take advantage of His promises to restore what is wrong in your home. In this segment, we will therefore look together at some Bible verses you as a woman can use to pray and expect to receive help from GOD.

1. Praying for attachment and torque unity

"Therefore, shall a man leave his father and mother, and shall cleave to his wife, and they shall become one flesh. **Genesis 2:24 (Mark 10:7; Ephesians 5:31; Matthew 19:5).**

Using this verse as an anchor scripture, you can pray in order to consolidate the unity of your couple, and to prevent any external influence that is not in conformity with the Word of GOD.

2. Praying against all negative family and ancestral influences

Based on the previous verse, since you now form one flesh with your husband, you can pray for separation from any unholy inherited family ties and/or any negative ancestral influences in your own family, as well as that of your husband.

3. Praying against any adulterous relationship and negative influence from the outside

The same verse says that they form one flesh, therefore, on your behalf and that of your husband, you as a wife can oppose any bond or door opened to the devil by sin and reestablish the reign of Christ in her marriage.

This also applies to all internal injuries that have occurred since childhood. You can pray not only for healing from your past, your memory, your subconscious; your heart, but also pray the same concerning your husband, since you are now one.

4. <u>Praying against all debauchery</u>

1 Corinthians 7:4 "*The wife has no authority over her own body, but the husband does; and likewise, the husband has no authority over his own body, but the wife does.*

On the strength of this verse, as wife, you can order in prayer, the body of your husband, not to take part in any kind of libertinage and pray that GOD will preserve him from it.

5. <u>Praying for her husband's favor:</u>

In Esther's time, whoever (including the queen) presented himself before the king without being invited risked death. However, after praying, Queen Esther appeared before the king without permission, at a time when the king no longer seemed to be too interested in her. However, the Lord inclined the king's heart in her favor and Esther was not beheaded, on the contrary, she was honored.

"All the king's servants and the people of his provinces know that any person, man or woman, who enters the king's house, in the inner court, without having been summoned, is entitled to only one verdict: death. The only person who remains alive is the one to whom the king hands the golden scepter. As far as I am concerned, it has been 30 days since I was called to him. **"Esther 4:11**.

*"When he saw Queen Esther standing in the court, she won his favor and he handed her the golden scepter he was holding. Esther approached and touched the end of the scepter. "*Esther **5:2.**

If your husband seems to turn away from you, GOD can turn his heart back to you. Ask the Lord for this grace in prayer.

Proverbs 21:1 *"The king's heart is a stream of water in the hand of the Lord; He inclines it wherever He wills"*.

6. <u>Praying for the conversion of her husband and children</u>

Acts 16:31 *"Paul and Silas answered, 'Believe in the Lord Jesus, and you will be saved, you and your family.*

As a woman, you can pray using this verse for the conversion of yourr family members.

Because of GOD's Covenant with David, all his descendants have been blessed by GOD. likewise, based on your own Covenant with GOD, you can ensure the continuity of the blessing on your descendants.

Chapitre III.   Ministry of Women Affairs

Many people feel the call of GOD but do not know exactly in which field not to what they are called for. They see themselves proclaiming the gospel to crowds, healing the sick in large assemblies, but do not know where or how to begin.

In general, between the time of the call, and the exercise of the ministry to which GOD calls us, there is distinctively, the time of training, and the time of service.

If you do not know how to surrender to GOD's service - and this concerns every called person - start by doing what you know GOD will always ask of you: joy, prayer and thanksgiving.

1 Thessalonians 5:16-18 *"Always be joyful. Pray without ceasing. Give thanks in all things, for this is the will of God in Christ Jesus for you.*

Pray to maintain your relationship with the Lord, pray for others; intercede for the nations; for the poor; for people who do not know GOD and for missionaries of the Gospel, so that evangelism may bear fruits. There is so much to do on your knees!!! Christians generally like to complain about circumstances, whereas what GOD expects from us is precisely to impact the world with our prayers and our radiance.

If you are faithful in what constitutes the general mission of every person on earth, GOD will reveal to you the specific one you are assigned to.

Thus, as a woman, the Lord entrusts to you a ministry, with very precise portfolio. Let us see here some fields of practice.

A. Being a wife and a mother: A Ministry established by the Lord

To the wife and mother, the first call of the Lord is displayed in her home. She represents the discreet but central regulatory element on which the Lord bases, through His Word, the stability and happiness of the family.

*"The wise woman builds her house, and the foolish woman knocks it down with her own hands. "***Proverbs 14:1.**

The woman receives from GOD a mission to accomplish: the building of her home. It is her responsibility to do so, first through prayer, then through education and the framework she creates within her home.

A sad and morose woman conveys the same atmosphere in her home, while a happy and serene woman reassures her whole family.

A mother devoted to prayer transmits to her children, her faith and her affection to the Lord.

2 Timothy 1:5 *"For I remember the sincere faith that is in you. It first dwelt in your grandmother Lois and your mother Eunice, and I am sure that it dwells in you as well.*

Far from us to say that a woman is to be blamed for the hard time her family go through. Remember that the devil is the accuser, and sole orchestrator to blame. The turmoil that can occur within the family unit can be the result of bad choices that others make. But through perseverance in prayer, the woman extends the pole of salvation to her entire family members. **Acts**

16:31 *"Paul and Silas answered, 'Believe in the Lord Jesus, and you and your family will be saved.*

To you women who are currently going through difficult times in your homes or families (misunderstandings; school failure; child addiction to drugs; alcohol and other substances...), do not lose hope. Continue to stand up in prayer against every spirit that causes this disorder and give thanks to the Lord for the deliverance He obtained for you on the cross, 2000 years ago. Never get tired of being thankful unto the Lord. Surely, He will bring you Victory over your enemies and restore the years that the devourer has stolen from you. Be strengthened in JESUS, Victory is yours for the taking!

I. <u>Mission: Intercession and supplication</u>

The woman's help first materializes in prayer.

The married woman must pray for her husband and children until she obtains from the Lord, a Word, a revelation, a promise that will serve as a support to continue to believe and stand firm in difficult times.

Prayer gets everything don!

In the face of certain challenges, it is up to the woman to roll up her sleeves and take up the fight in a praying posture, as Hannah the mother of Samuel did. **1 Samuel 1.**

There was an issue in her home. Hannah was unable to give birth and was mocked by her rival Peninna, who had several sons and daughters. This situation was very trying for her, although she had the grace to have a supportive husband throughout the ordeal, who tried to make her forget it. The Bible says that Elkana, Hannah's husband loved her, even though JEHOVAH had made her barren. Note: Many women today do not benefit from this same level of understanding but, they can count on the support of Him who made heaven and earth, His support alone to you is enough to change your story and that of your family. Amen.

Let me challenge at this point, our sisters in the Lord, by saying that one cannot use a child to hold a man, it is an illusion. It is JEHOVAH who lays the foundations of a couple, not any constraint. Love is not born of a trap!

Hannah's story is really inspiring in that:

First, the Bible says that JEHOVAH had made her barren. If GOD Himself makes you barren, then who will give you a child? Such situation is more than desperate because when GOD closes the Door, no one can open it.

In addition, the Bible recalls that each year, the family made a pilgrimage to the house of the Lord, as commanded in Israel. Elkanah, her husband, through his sacrifices to the LORD, worshipped Him faithfully, despite the painful reproach of his wife's bareness. It was a family devoted in prayer. They had certainly presented this situation to the Lord hundreds of times.

But notice with me that something special happened when Anne took over. I like this version of **1 Samuel 1:9-10** which says, "*This time, after they had eaten and drunk in Shiloh, Hannah arose and went to the sanctuary of the LORD... Grieving greatly, Hannah prayed to the LORD weeping with tears.*

On other occasions, Anne prayed, but this time she stood up resolutely, with the firm intention of going out to meet and touch the heart of GOD, the One who makes fruitful. Result: the miracle happened!!! She became pregnant and gave birth to Samuel.

Instead of feeling sorry for ourselves, complaining and accusing the Lord, we ought to rise in prayer and go to meet our GOD. Something extraordinary will happen and the locks will give way.

II. <u>Mission : Pray and fight</u>

The Bible says in **Revelation 12:12,** *"Therefore rejoice, O heavens, and you who dwell in the heavens. Woe to the earth and to the sea! For the devil has come down to you in great wrath, knowing that he has but a short time.'* Now the book of Genesis speaks of a perpetual battle between the woman, her descendants and the devil. *"I will put enmity between the woman and you, between her seed and yours. And hers shall crush your head, and you shall bite her on the heel* " **Genesis 3:15.**

It is therefore a serious and relentless fight woman must wage for their homes; their husbands and children, for if every family is blessed, the whole society will be blessed.

One only has to look at the number of families torn apart and the number of lives turned upside down as a result of family problems and the repercussions of difficult childhood, to understand that these numbers are pointers to the fact that families are under attack by the devil.

Do you know that the devil can see the star of someone called to a great mission in the work of GOD? If that person cannot be accessible to him, he will attempt to go through that person's future husband/wife to harm him or her. That is to say, he will try to drag the future spouse into vices or bonds, so much so that later on, in the home, that person will not have the time to be dedicated to the mission, by the result of the torments inflicted by the partner. This is the reason why, as believers who has received the call, we must constantly pray for our spouses (even if we do not know them yet). If you are not yet married or even engaged, you should not hesitate to fast and pray for the deliverance; conversion; devotion to the Lord; consecration ... of your spouse. Your future serenity depends on it!

In the same way, in the home, instead of constantly accusing the counterpart and becoming discouraged, you should rather show compassion towards your husband, discerning that he is under the influence of the evil one, because of his great destiny or yours! Pray without ceasing for your spouse and show him/her love!

2 Corinthians 2:5-8 "If anyone *has been a cause of sorrow, [...]. It is enough for that man to have been blamed [...]; therefore, now you must rather forgive him and encourage him, so that too much sadness does not lead him to despair. Therefore, I ask you, give him proof of your love for him.*

III. <u>Mission: To bring to the world the Love it needs</u>

The world is crying out for Love and it is the responsibility of women to bring this Love to the scene.

Some people know JESUS but have not experienced His Love. They are wounded Christians, yet prisoners of hope whose thirst can only be quenched by GOD's Love.

The Bible urges (4 times) husbands to love their wives: **Colossians 3:19**, **Ephesians 5:25, 28 and 33**. This is probably because the Lord knows that Love is already innate in the woman. He does not need to demand so much for her t manifest it, because she has this capacity to be sensitive to the sufferings of others, to witness much love and perseverance. The woman is endowed with natural gentleness, sensitivity and compassion. These aptitudes dispose her to listen to others and to bring them comfort and peace!

The Love of a mother is unconditional, despite the disappointments, ingratitude and rebellions of her children. *"Does a woman forget the child she is breastfeeding? Does she not pity the fruit of her womb? When she forgets it, I will not forget you.* **Isaiah 49:15.**

And what about the love of a wife?

The woman must realize that her role goes beyond the boundaries of her small family. It is our duty to bring to the world, the Love and the consolation it so many needs.

It can be in charitable works, through simple visits to the loneliest and/or destitute people, bringing an attentive ear to people battered by grief and giving them hope.

The consoling ability of the woman is such that the Lord Himself uses her as a reference: *"As a man whom his mother comforts, so will I comfort you....* **"Isaiah 49:15.**

So, do not neglect yourself! You have much to contribute to humanity: love; compassion; consolation; restoration; life…!

IV. <u>Mission : To give life</u>

The woman as a mother has within her the capacity to give life physically, but also spiritually. Her body is made to carry and mature the fertilized egg into a living, viable baby. In the same way, spiritually, she carries within her the necessary attributes to make the invisible 'mustard seed' GOD has planted in the life of her husband and children grow into glorious vessels of honor for the Lord and whose fruits will serve generations.

Indeed, each person comes into the world with a potential triggered by the likeness of the Lord in him. Even those we believe to be very evil, have a seed of GOD in them, which is only waiting to be nurtured to the point of giving birth to transformation.

Matthew 5:44-46 *"But I say to you, Love your enemies, [bless those who curse you, do good to those who hate you] and pray for those [who] abuse and persecute you, that you may be sons of your heavenly Father. For He makes His sun to shine on righteous and the unrighteous. If you love those who love you, what reward do you deserve? ..."*.

Just as it is not a woman's responsibility to determine the ingredients of her breast milk, or how it will grow the baby she breastfeeds, it is not a woman's responsibility to transform her husband or children. Many women exhaust

themselves trying to transform their husbands and shape their children. It is not your role!

You do not need to know how many vitamins breast milk contains, and exactly what it will be used for in the baby's growth process. Whether you know it or not, breast milk contributes exactly what the baby needs. Whether the child is healthy or deficient in iron, magnesium, vitamin D, etc., the same milk will meet the child's needs as they appear, without any extra effort on the mother's part. This happens almost automatically.

Therefore, the woman must simply create the necessary framework for the gestation of the seed, nourish it with spiritual mother's milk and "*leave no room for the devil*" Ephesians 4:27.

It will simply be a matter of bringing the person before the Lord, in prayer, with faith and perseverance, in order to see the miracle blossom. Growth, therefore, comes in an atmosphere bathed in the presence of GOD through a life dedicated to thanksgiving and praise.

1 Samuel 2:21 " *... And the young Samuel grew up with the Lord.* »

Luke 2:40 "*And the child [JESUS] grew and was strengthened [in spirit]. He was full of wisdom and the grace of God was upon him.*

V. <u>Mission: Bringing the world a solution</u>

At the entrance of the Lycée Sainte Marie de Cocody (Côte d'Ivoire), a girls high school where I did all my secondary education, there is an insignia: **"To raise a man is to raise a person, to raise a woman is to raise a nation".**

Hannah, in giving birth to Samuel, did not only find a solution to her sterility problem. She also wished to bring a solution to the spiritual barrenness afflicting Israel; for the Bible says in **1 Samuel 3:1** that *"the Word of JEHOVAH was scarce at that time"*. So, the Lord answered her. Further on, in **verse 20,** it is said that in all Israel, Samuel was recognized as a prophet, because JEHOVAH left none of his words without effect. Israel had a Prophet! As for Hannah, the Lord gave her more children.

As Christians, we are called to impact the world and bring to it the flavor and light it needs. Doesn't JESUS say, *"You are the salt of the earth and the light of the world? "*»

We do not have to wait to be asked. Our capacity to observe should lead us to discern the areas in which Divine intervention is needed, and to bring in GOD's favor and blessing through prayer and works.

This is exactly what happened at the wedding at Cana in **John 2.** Mary observed that wine was finished, so she intervened on behalf of the couple, then the miracle took place, for the happiness of all. We too must intercede for others, without them even knowing that we are praying for them. In this way, our reward will be great in heaven.

So many people are suffering and are on the verge of depression because they don't know JESUS, and are ignorant of the fact that out of love for them, He went to the extent of dying the most infamous death ever seen: the death on the cross, so that they may have life, in abundance. People are slaves to all kinds of vices and since the world cannot find solutions to eradicate these evils, it prefers to legalize them; to authorize them, to legitimize what everyone knows is bad for Man. Meanwhile, the Christians who carry within them the light, that is Jesus Christ Who has the power to break all the chains of slavery, indulge in pedantic speeches and other distractions instead of proclaiming Him.

1 Corinthians 2:4 *"My word and my preaching was not based on persuasive words of [human] wisdom, but on a demonstration of the Spirit and power.*

Worse still, some Christians hide their dread of expressing their faith behind the pretext of fear or freedom of others, when the Bible states clearly that "we have not received a spirit of timidity." It is time for us to bring to the world; to all the people in distress, the truth of the Gospel: The Mighty JESUS of 2000 years ago, for He has not changed. People's freedom will then be expressed in that they will have the choice to believe it or not. Nonetheless, at least let us bring them the Good News!

More and more, Christians glory in the inter-church movements and/or prayer groups they create around them. Instead of trying to recruit in our prayers and assemblies, people already converted whom we can see know the Lord (because it is easier), let us not be afraid to go on missions. Let us go fishing for lost souls stuck in the hell of drugs; alcohol; prostitution; homosexuality; pedophilia; kleptomania and so on. This is what GOD is calling us to!

"...Much will be demanded from the one to whom much has been given, and more will be demanded from the one to whom much has been entrusted. **"Luke 12:48.**

"Therefore, the creation longs for the revelation of the sons of God" **Romans 8:19.**

The Lord's last recommendation was this: "... *Go into all the world and preach the good news to all creation".* **Mark 16:15.**

By giving priority to the affairs of the Kingdom, we commit GOD to take care of us: *"Seek first the Kingdom of heaven and its righteousness.*

Woman take your pilgrim's staff and go and share the Love of Christ to the world!

Start with small things around you, and do not be afraid to go further. Go with the strength that you have; JEHOVAH will sustain you.

Judges 6:14: *"The Lord turned to him, and said, 'Go with this strength that you have, and deliver Israel out of the hand of Midian; did not I send you? ".*

B.   The Laws of the Righteous Woman

I. <u>The Law of Honor</u>

When the Lord created man, He commanded him to rule the earth. There is therefore in every man this natural tendency to want to rule and this instinctive need to mark his territory; to feel respected and honored.

Thus, if there is only one place on earth where your husband must find his honor; his respect; his dignity, it is as he returns home; by your side and with your children. Life's difficulties, failures; struggles; wickedness often suffocate man in his daily interactions with the outside world. His home is the Place given to him by the Lord to express his leadership potential and to regain his honor.

Some women mistakenly see the expression of this potential as a challenge and engage in a wrestling match with their husbands. This is a lost fight because the Lord will not support you.

GOD Himself established man as head of the family, and this should not be forgotten.

Ephesians 5:21 *"For the husband is the head of the wife, even as Christ is the head of the church, which is her body, of which he is the Savior.*

The Bible speaks of Sarah as a virtuous woman who called her husband "my master" **1 Peter 3:6.**

This may seem a bit excessive from a human point of view, but if we put ourselves in the framework set out above, we understand that there is nothing excessive about honoring one's husband as a master.

The Bible asks men to love their wives as JESUS loved the church to the point of giving his life for her! Women will find this very "romantic" while men will find it excessive...And yet, this is the Divine commandment!

This last image is more excessive than the first one concerning Sarah, because it sets the scene for a bride who, like the Church, obeys and submits herself without limit or reserve to her Lord JESUS and yet, this is the Divine commandment!

As Christians, we do not have to sanction what pleases us only and condemn what seems to us a little excessive in the precepts of the Lord. We just must adhere and obey. The world may call us stupid; naive, and even our conscience may suggest that we are being exploited by people who think they are smarter than we are. Regardless, we know whom we have put our trust in. The patriarchs of the Bible did not shine by their conformity to the logic of this world, but rather by their Faith and obedience to the will of GOD, stand that seemed foolish in the eyes of men.

<u>A few examples</u>:

Abraham who abandons everything: family; stability ... and leaves for an unknown country, not even clearly determined at the time of departure!

Genesis 12:1" *The LORD said to Abram, "Go from your land, from your homeland, and from your father's house, into the <u>land that I will show you</u>.*

Joshua and the people of Israel, who at the time of taking possession of Jericho, by order of the Lord, went round the walls instead of preparing a military strategy. **Joshua 6**.

JESUS, to heal the blind man from birth, applies to his eyes mud that he made with his saliva!

John 9:6 *"When he had said this, he spat on the ground, and made mud with his spittle. Then he applied the mud to the eyes of the blind man.*

Obedience to GOD's ordinances always assures man the perfect blessing.

The problem is that Man tends to reason, and under the pretext of what seems right to him, does not do what GOD asks, but true justice is determined by GOD!

Stop saying "it's fair" or "it's not fair." Just obey GOD and you will preserve your life for He will take care of your interests. As my spiritual father often says, let us stop being assistant-gods, let's stay in our place as men and leave it to GOD to be GOD.

"Such a way seems right to a man, but the way out is the way of death." **Proverbs 16:25** and **Proverbs 14:12**.

Moreover, the Wisdom of GOD has nothing in comparison with the thoughts of Men. It supersedes it.

1 Corinthians 3:19 *"For the wisdom of this world is foolishness before God.*

1 Corinthians 1:25 *"For the foolishness of God is wiser than men, and the weakness of God is stronger than men.*

Furthermore, endorsing a child's lack of respect for his or her father (by encouraging the act or simply by silence) makes us accomplice in the curse that the child is undergoing. *"Honor thy father and thy mother, that thy days may be prolonged in the land which the LORD thy God giveth thee.* **"Exodus 20:12**.

Note that it says, "honor your father and your mother", not your righteous; perfect; Christian father etc.

It is true that some parents under the influence of the devil in their lives, are real threats to their children. These cases, which are fortunately rare, are peculiar and therefore deserve the intervention of an authorized councilor.

In ordinary cases, it is good to remember that this Divine Command is not optional. Differences of opinion; misunderstandings, even parental shortcomings are not sufficient reasons to evade it. The same is true of the duty to obey the parents.

"For Moses said, "Respect your father and mother", and "Whoever curses his father or mother must be put to death". But you, you teach that if a man says to his father or his mother: "What I could give you to help you is Corban" - that is, "offering reserved for God" - he no longer needs to do anything for his father or his mother, you allow him to do so. In this way, you cancel the requirement of the word of God through the tradition you transmit. And you do many other similar things". **Mark 7 :10-13**.

II. <u>The law of diligence and courage</u>

Proverbs 31:10-31 portrays the virtuous woman. *We will resume this beautiful text at the end of the book.*

The Bible presents her as a woman who does not eat the bread of laziness; gets up early to work with energy and never leaves her hands idle.

A virtuous woman is diligent. This shows clearly that the Lord is no supporter of the least effort, but on the contrary, He rewards the brave.

Woman, you who fight daily for the well-being of your family, be strengthened and blessed in the Name of JESUS. Know that the Lord sees your efforts and He will crown you in the eyes of all when the time comes, provided you do not give up.

Proverbs 31:31 " "*Many women are valiant," he says, "but you surpass them all." Charm is deceptive, beauty is fleeting, only a woman who is submissive to the Lord is worthy of praise. Reward her for her trouble! Let her merits be sung in public squares! "*».

III. <u>The law of self-giving</u>

According to **1 Corinthians 7:4,** "*The wife has no authority over her own body, but the husband does; and likewise, the husband has no authority over his own body, but the wife does.*

Thus, in marriage, the wife's body belongs to her husband and vice versa. They must not deny each other. This is a prescription. Of course, as Christians, we must pray that the devil will not use this truth to lead us into vices and other deviations. For example, the husband cannot under the pretext that his wife's body belongs to him, subject her to practices of swinging or prostitution etc. It is said that they do not deny each <u>other</u> and not people.

1 Corinthians 7:5 *"Do not refuse one another unless you agree to do so momentarily to devote yourselves to prayer; but then return to normal married life, otherwise you risk losing control of yourself and giving in to the temptations of Satan.*

IV. <u>The Law of Joy and Thanksgiving</u>

1 Samuel 1:18 *" "And she said, "And you, keep your lovingkindness to me. Ann went away and agreed to eat. The sadness was gone from her face.*

As soon as Hannah finished presenting her petition to the Lord, she moved on. The sadness left her face and she agreed to eat. The Lord honored her faith and she became pregnant.

You must know how to move on and trust in the Lord. Moreover, a continually sad face attracts an unpleasant atmosphere in the house.

2 Kings 4:17-36 The Shunamite woman is an excellent example of joy and faith. During her trial, she remained serene and diligent despite the sorrow that filled her soul because of the death of her only son, born after all hope of giving birth was lost. She is careful not to panic and tells her husband that

<u>everything is fine</u>. Then she goes to meet the Prophet of GOD because she knows that the solution is in GOD. In the end, the Lord honored her faith and her son came back to life.

Joy is not necessarily expressed, but it is the ability to not get depressed, and not make one's environment sink into sadness, by means of an active Faith.

2 Kings 4:16 " *He asked, "Why do you want to go to him today? It is neither the beginning of the month nor the Sabbath. " And she said, "It's all right. "*

2 Kings 4:27 " *... Elisha said to him, "Leave her alone! She is filled with a sadness of which I know not the cause, for God has not made it known to me." ».*

2 Kings 4:36 " *Elisha called Gehazi and said to him, "Call our Sunamite. " Gehazi called her and she came to Elisha who said, "Take your son! "''».*

1 Thessalonians 5:16 *"Always be joyful.*

The Bible speaks of garments of praise. May praise become your way of life!

V. <u>The Law of trust</u>

Man is not infallible, it is true. However, when a couple enters marriage before GOD, they are no longer two but one flesh, **anchored in Christ**. Therefore, GOD's blessing and favor accompanies this union, because of the tripartite Covenant which is automatically sealed.

Also, the trust we place (still) in the future of our home, is not focused on the spouse, but on our trust in this Faithful GOD, who has made this marriage possible and is committed to walk with us.

So, when we have been through a big storm of disappointment, it is important to pray that the trust we had in our loved one be restored. Nobody is perfect, starting with us, and the wounds we sometimes inflict on ourselves in the home can create reluctance to 'embrace'. In this case, it is advisable to pray, to obtain from GOD the grace to forgive and forget, in order to foster a climate of trust necessary for the stability of the couple.

Some women, in addition to being inquisitive, are excessively jealous and create an unbearable climate in the home for a yes or no answer. By doing so, you show your husband that you do not trust him, and this can frustrate him. Moreover, you are telling GOD that you want to manage your fights yourself when He has promised to fight for you.

You need to understand that the fight is not about your husband's phone, or the "secrets" he seems to hide. You do not even need to know who is a potential "threat" to your relationship.

Israel did not need to know what Balak was plotting against them with the help of the soothsayer Balaam! But at the right time, JEHOVAH prevented the curse from reaching His children. **Numbers chapters 22- 24.**

Do not weary yourself any more my daughter, and enter rest, for your GOD fights for you!

VI. <u>The law of forgiveness, love and temperance.</u>

2 Corinthians 2:5-8 "*If anyone has been a cause of sorrow, [...]. It is enough for that man to have been blamed [...]; therefore, now you must rather forgive him and encourage him, so that too much sadness does not lead him to despair. Therefore, I ask you, give him proof of your love for him.*"

As seen above, it is essential to ensure that the atmosphere in the house is peaceful and pleasant. Also, when there are things to reproach the spouse for, the Bible recommends that we say them and then forgive. Moreover, the Gospel goes so far as to recommend that the sun should not set on our anger. **Still, the virtuous woman must have enough self-control not** to act or respond under the effect of anger; but wait until the storm is passed, to be sure to produce the desired effect.

Temperance and forgiveness are necessary for a peaceful atmosphere in the house. Some women complain about their husbands' excessive outbursts, but who wants to cohabit with unfounded quarrels?

4 verses of the Bible take up the same idea:

Proverbs 17:1 "*Better a piece of dry bread with peace than a house full of meat with quarrels*".

Proverbs 21:19 "It is *better to live in a desert land than with a quarrelsome and irritable woman.*

Proverbs 25:24 "It is *better to live at the corner of a roof than to make a house together with a quarrelsome woman.*

Proverbs 21:9 "It is *better to live in the corner of a roof than to make a house together with a quarrelsome woman.*

Sure, you do not ask a woman to be a blessed yes-yes and say nothing. But a remark or a complaint can very well be expressed calmly. Moreover, a complaint formulated wisely, calmly, at the right time, has much more effect and a lot of chances of being listened to.

The tranquility of a house is maintained by the mistress of the house.

Proverbs 31:27 *"She watches over her house.*

VII.<u>The Law of Fidelity</u>

We have seen from our above analysis, that marriage is a divine institution GOD demands to be honored by all.

Hebrews 13:4 *"Let marriage be honored by all, and the marriage bed be made clean, for God will judge whoever commits fornication and adultery. »*

GOD cannot ask us to honor something that He Himself does not approve of and does not defend.

As much as the bride and groom must honor their own marriage, so must those around them, and not encourage the spouses to turn away from this recommendation. Indeed, this verse is unequivocal and prohibits all forms of adultery, even by mutual agreement. Extra-marital relations; exchanges between consenting spouses; so-called "free" marriages and others are tricks of the devil to lead the children of GOD to oppose the will of the Father and consequently, draw them into hell with him.

"Know this well: No immoral, unclean or stingy being (for greed is idolatry) will ever share in the Kingdom of Christ and God.

Let no one lead you astray by deceptive reasoning: it is such faults that bring God's wrath upon those who oppose Him" **Ephesians 5:6-7.**

C.   Some attitudes to avoid

I am used to saying: <u>Be careful not to do the right things for the wrong reasons</u>.

Proverbs 4:23 *"Above all, be careful what you think within yourself, for your life depends on it.*

At this level, it is important to remember that everything we do must be done with the Lord in mind, and for His Glory. All the recommendations previously mentioned must be implemented in this spirit otherwise, doing these things and thinking or wishing the opposite completely negates all our efforts, because our GOD knows everything: *"He searches the hearts and the loins"* **Psalms 7:9 (7:10).**

A distinction must be made between the total surrender to GOD referred to here, and any sense of contentment that the devil might inspire, for such a negative feeling produces frustration; resentment; contempt and finally recrimination for what GOD has given as Ministry and Blessing.

We are going to review those attitudes that could be an obstacle to our entry into the 'Promised Land', obstacles that **must be avoided at all costs.**

I. <u>Sadness and contentment :</u>

It is not a question of performing acts of kindness with deep down in one's heart, sadness or a feeling of helplessness, contentment or spite.

Already, this will wear you down very quickly and this feeling will turn into anger, exasperation or contempt.

In fact, it is every time the same principle that the enemy uses from the Garden of Eden (**Genesis 3)** to this day: to question the immeasurable, incomparable, infinite and extraordinary Love of GOD for you and I. Certainly the greatest offense we can do to the Fatherly heart of our GOD is to doubt His Love for us, despite the daily manifestations of His faithfulness (which we trivialize and/or take for granted).

"The Lord said to Moses: "How long will this people despise me? How long will they not believe in me, despite all the signs that I have done in their midst? I will strike them with pestilence and destroy them, but I will make you a nation greater and more powerful than him". **Numbers 14: 11-12**.

More often than not, when a Christian woman is engaged in a faith process concerning her marriage, a faith based on the Word of GOD, the enemy tries to give her the impression that her efforts are in vain; that she is tiring herself out for nothing; that the person opposite is making no effort or that she does not deserve to make all these sacrifices. Sometimes, the devil does not hesitate to push the envelope even further by sending particularly "interesting" suitors to her entourage or simply by putting her on a high social level that would justify her contempt for a husband, who, moreover, would be mean.

That may be true, your husband may be mean, surely selfish, even ungrateful... and he does not really deserve to be bent over backwards for him when you make that observation. Sometimes even, the harder you try, the tougher the other person before you will become, or the more rejection you will be victim of, which can be deeply hurtful. In such cases, in order not to become discouraged and give up, we should remember that **Christ loved us while we were still sinners and did not deserve His sacrifice.**

Matthew 5:44-46 *"But I say to you, Love your enemies, [bless those who curse you, do good to those who hate you] and pray for those [who] abuse and persecute you, that you may be sons of your heavenly Father. For He makes His sun rise on the wicked and on the good, and rains on the righteous and on the unrighteous. If you love those who love you, what reward do you deserve? ..."*.

Romans 5:8 *"But God proves his love for us, in that, while we were still sinners, Christ died for us.*

In fact, when one understands that marriage is a ministry, he or she behaves like the missionary who goes to remote areas to proclaim the Gospel. Although the expression of gratitude on the part of those visited would be of great comfort, the missionary does not make it a vital requirement, for he knows that his reward will come to him from the Lord, first on this earth and then in heaven when he dies.

So, rather than allowing herself to be distracted and saddened by the difficulties of marriage, the woman must remember that in the Kingdom of GOD's children, Faith precedes sight, unlike the world that sees before believing. One must persevere and continue to believe in this GOD of the Covenant, for His Faithfulness is never lacking and lasts forever.

It is at this moment that we must put into practice all our potential of faith, hope and trust in the Heavenly Father who loves us above all else and who wants our good. We must remember the Lord's promises, remember them and proclaim positive words. Personally, this is my method when discouragement or weariness knocks at the door of my heart, I declare this: "Satan leave me alone, you are a liar, you are defeated. Let JEHOVAH rebuke thee! Then I go on saying: "Thank you Lord because You do everything for my good and happiness. I thank You because You are the GOD of the Covenant and Your promise always comes true !!! »

Finally, I reflect on what I know to be GOD's will: To be always joyful, and thankful. **1 Thessalonians 5:16**.

Usually this leads me to a moment of thanksgiving or praise. What is great about this method is that it can be applied anywhere, at work, on the street, on the bus... everywhere. And above all, the fruits are immediate and very often visible and contagious!!!

II. <u>Contempt</u>

It often happens after a long wait without results. After a long series of frustrations, inner wounds, love turns into hatred and/or contempt. More so because, having lived with your husband, you know his unwelcoming sides. However, no matter what limitations your spouse, like any other person, may have, you must never come to contempt.

Contempt, even if it is not expressed, behaves like a gangrene that gnaws at us from within and robs us of our joy and hope. Moreover, if you despise your husband, it will drive him away because he will eventually feel it.

What a wife must above all avoid is denigrating her husband, whether in public; in private; in front of him or without his knowledge, in his absence, and even demeaning him in her heart.

Just remember: We owe respect and submission to our spouses. How can we respect; help; love someone we despise even secretly, in the depth of our heart?

If the years of disappointments and wounds… have led you today to contempt, I invite you to make this prayer with me now:

"Lord JESUS, I come humbly to Thee. You know my heart and You know how wounded it is. I am aware of the contempt that has invaded it and I would like to ask You for forgiveness. Come by Your blood, deliver me from this hatred that imprisons me and fill me with Your love. I no longer want to see my husband's shortcomings, but rather grasp how wonderful You have created him! May I respect, cherish and honor my

*husband. May I be able to fully play my role as wife, friend, confidant and helper **to** him for Your Glory, in JESUS name! Amen"*.

III. <u>Complaints, negative thoughts and words</u>

Imagine that you give your child a gift you have spent a lot of money on, and without even unwrapping it, he starts to sulk, complain, grumble, simply because he doesn't like the gift wrap, or it has been tied tightly, in such a way that the child has a little trouble opening it. One remark; then two, it could pass. But after 45 minutes of complaining and even accusations; questioning of the genuineness of your love worse, insults..., you would be tempted to get angry, take back the gift from him, frustrated by the fact that beyond not appreciating the present, he doesn't trust that you as a parent want the best for him.

JESUS says: *"You who are wicked know how to give good things to your children, how much more so does your Father who is in heaven.* **Matthew 7:11.**

Remember, recrimination is a favorite weapon of the deceiver. It is the weapon he used in the wilderness, to prevent the children of GOD ([1st] generation) from entering the promised land of Canaan!

In the same way, recrimination could deny you the blessing of happiness promised by our GOD.

We are human and such reaction, can temptingly punctuate our journey on the path to heaven, our promised land. It is then necessary to remember that this attitude is not inspired by GOD but instigated by the evil one.

If years of disappointments, injuries etc. have engendered negative thoughts and led you to complain and recriminate against the Lord, I invite you to pray the following with me now:

*"Lord JESUS, I come humbly to Thee. You know my heart and You know how wounded it is. I am aware of the contempt that has invaded it and I would like to ask You for forgiveness. I ask You to forgive me for all these negative thoughts I have harbored ; for all the wicked words I spat to my husband's face; for all the complaints and accusations I have made before You instead of praying to You in trust and thanksgiving. I cancel today all these thoughts and words in the Name of JESUS. Come, cleans me by Your blood! Deliver me O Lord, from this hatred that imprisons me and fill me with Your love. I no longer want to see the inadequacies of my husband, but rather focus on the wonderful way You have created him! May I respect, cherish and honor my husband. May I be able to fully play my role as wife, friend, confidante, and helper **to** him, for Your Glory, in JESUS name! Amen".*

To conclude this part: *"Watch over your heart more than anything else, because your life depends on it"*. **Proverbs 4 :23**.

IV. <u>Gossiping, taking dirty laundry outside...</u>

Proverbs 13:3 *"He that watches over his mouth keeps his soul; he that opens wide his lips runs to his ruin.*

It may seem difficult, but if the Lord demand it from the woman, it is because He has given her the strength to be able to do it!

Some women make the mistake of exposing to their best friends, or even their parents, the slightest discussion in the home, subjecting everything to their opinions. Consequently, instead of being a couple who build their decisions on the Lord, the duo end up becoming a trio, a quartet etc...

This can be frustrating for the spouse who sees his or her life exposed and victimized by the advice of outsiders.

For this reason, we strongly dissuade women from reporting all household disputes outside the marital home in the exception of a spiritual father, who has the duty to pray and advice in cases of violence or exposure to certain danger.

It is said that "*Mary kept all these things and pondered them in her heart. "* **Luke 2:19.**

The first reason is simple: what binds you to your spouse is Love. A Love that should be strong enough to protect the 'one flesh tie'. This Love is endowed with the capacity to forgive and forget after reconciliation. The second reason on the other hand, is that despite the affection your entourage may have for your spouse; their patience has its limits, and long after the reconciliations, forgiveness and forgetfulness may be difficult.

Finally, this assertion is based on the fundamental principle that **life and death are in the power of words.**

   Proverbs 18:21 "*Tongue has power of life and death; those who love to speak will taste its fruits.*

What we declare is what we see happening in our lives. Has not the Lord made man in His likeness, man and woman?

This implies that we have the same creative power as our Father (at least in part). That is the reason why Man is capable of inventing and putting to the service of the community, discoveries each one more extraordinary than the other.

We know that the mind is the womb of every inventions. In other words, what we can call into existence and create finds its origin in our thoughts and imagination.

The Bible says that "out of *the abundance of the heart the mouth speaks*. So, whether you are aware of it or not, what you say, even in jest, comes from an abundance of your heart, and has the power to create something as repercussion.

Proverbs 21:23 "*He who watches over his mouth and his tongue preserves his soul from anguish.*

V. <u>Do not separate what GOD has joined together:</u>

"*Let not man therefore separate that which GOD has joined together*". **Mark 10:9.**

The warning is clear. It applies to all: family, friends, and to everyone who indulge in fleeting relationships though aware of the married status of the counterpart. Indeed, the great risk here is falling under the judgment of a GOD who is the defender of the Covenant to which HE has committed Himself. If it is true that the Lord demands not to break the covenant He has made, it is because any contravention of this injunction bring automatically upon the culprit consequences. Let us remember Abimelech, whom we spoke of earlier. **Genesis 20:18** says that

"... the *LORD had brought barrenness upon all the house of Abimelech for Sarah, Abraham's wife.*

Here again, the aim is not to enter accusing judgments, but rather, to review our situation and if need be, repent and ask GOD humbly to help us, because no one is perfect.

I do not think, despite the appearances one would like to paint, that some women voluntarily decide to take on the position of mistress if they have not been victim of betrayal, sentimental failure or simply discouragement in the face of the passage of time. It is GOD who heals wounded hearts. He will act if we ask Him to. As Master of circumstances and time, He is never late to accomplish the best in our lives.

At this point, I would like to recall what we said earlier, that it is particularly important to discern one's vocation, and that happiness does not depend on any kind of marriage. If these points have been taken care of, then our legitimate expectation will be fulfilled by the Lord. He is Powerful to act, even when Men say it is too late.

The most telling example is that of the about 60-year aged Sarah, Abraham's wife - usually at this age, women despair of getting married - Sarah is courted by a king, and not the least of them: Abimelech, king of Gerar, whose kingdom was a very great military and economic power in its days, so much so that Abimelech had her kidnapped. **Genesis 20:2**.

The Favor of GOD can despite your advanced age, make you enter the joys of marriage!

Genesis 18:11 says that *"Abraham and Sarah were old and of advanced years, and Sarah could not hope to have children'*. However, at the age of 90 years old, Sarah gave birth, according to the promise of JEHOVAH.

I often say in my teachings that when GOD announces something, it is not because HE is looking for someone to help Him realize it, but rather because HE is Almighty to do so. He just needs people to believe Him and see Him fulfill His promises....

If GOD has promised you something, wait for it, for His Word will certainly be fulfilled.

Genesis 21:6-7" *Sarah said, "God made me laugh for joy. Everyone who hears about Isaac will laugh with me." And she added: "Who could have told Abraham that Sarah would one day nurse children? Yet I gave her a son in her old age. "*

VI. <u>Encourage the tried and tested</u>

It can often be revolting to see loved ones "suffer" in a beating relationship.

But the Bible says in **Numbers 13:32-33,** *"And they denigrated before the Israelites the land which they had explored. They said, "The land we have travelled through to explore it is a land that devours its inhabitants. All the people we saw there are tall men. We saw the giants, the descendants of Anak who came from the giants. To us and to them, we were like locusts. ""* ».

Numbers 14:1 "And *all the congregation rose up and shouted, and the people wept in the night.*

Numbers 32: 7-10 "*Why do you want to discourage the Israelites from passing through the land which the LORD gives them? This is what your fathers did when I sent them from Kadesh-Barnea to examine the land. They went up to the Valley of Eshcol, and after examining the land, they discouraged the Israelites from going into the land that the LORD gave them. The anger of the Lord was kindled that day and he swore.*

You are not aware of GOD's specific promises and plans for a couple. In time of doubt, when that couple is going through difficulties, the right attitude to adopt is to pray and intercede on their behalf. Moreover, the ordeal is already cause enough for discouragement, so they need reassurance, words of comfort instead. Once again, we are speaking under the reservation of a normal situation, that is, in the absence of a definite threat to the life of one or both partners.

"He doesn't break the already bent reed, he doesn't turn off the fading lamp..." **Isaiah 42:3.**

VII. <u>To consider oneself indispensable in a couple's happiness</u>

To consider oneself indispensable in a couple's happiness is literally taking the place of the Lord. GOD shares His Glory with no one. If you have such an attitude, the Lord will take it upon Himself to find you someone who, like you, will influence your home from the outside. Does He not say this?

Luke 6:31 *"Whatever you want men to do for you, do the same for them.*

Luke 6:38 *"For with what measure you measure it will be measured to you in return. "*» ?

Conclusion

In conclusion, I pray that women take their GOD given position not only in the family circle, but also in the society, in such a way that the blessing of JEHOVAH can rest upon all the families of the world, as **Numbers 6:22-27** declares:

"And *the Lord spoke to Moses, saying:*

23 Speak to Aaron and to his sons, and say, thus shall you bless the children of Israel, and say to them:

24 May the Lord bless you and keep you.

25 May the Lord make his face shine on you and give you his grace.

26 May the Lord turn his face to you and give you peace!

27 So they will put my name on the children of Israel, and I will bless them.

Amen.

The Righteous Woman - Proverbs 31:10-31

10 A valiant woman is a real find! She is more valuable than pearls.

11 Her husband puts his trust in her, and she does not waste her property on him.

12 She never does him any harm but gives him joy all the days of his life.

13 She gets wool and linen and works with her hands in earnest.

14 Like the merchant ships, she brings her food from afar.

15 She gets up before daylight, and prepares food for her family, and gives her maids their work.

16 When she had thought it over, she bought a field and planted a vineyard with the money she had earned.

17 She goes to work energetically and never leaves her arms idle.

18 She sees that her business is going well; she even works at night by the light of her lamp.

19 His hands are busy spinning wool, his fingers weaving clothes.

20 She extends a helping hand to the needy; she is generous to the poor.

21 She has no fear of the cold for her own, for everyone in her house has double clothing.

22 She makes carpets for herself and wears fine purple linen garments.

23 Her husband is an honorable notable; he participates in the council of the city.

24 She makes garments and sells them and delivers belts to the passing merchant.

25 Strength and dignity are her adornment, she smiles as she thinks of the future.

26 She speaks wisely and gives good advice.

27 She watches everything that happens in her house and refuses to remain inactive.

28 Her children come to congratulate her. Her husband sings her praises.

29 "Many women are valiant," he said, "but you are better than all of them. »

30 Charm is deceptive, beauty is fleeting, only a woman who is submissive to the Lord is worthy of praise.

31 Let him be rewarded for his trouble! Let his merits be sung in public squares!

About the author

Mimyelle is married and has wonderful children.

From a young age, she encountered the Lord in a very profound way and did not hesitate to integrate the charismatic renewal and the choir in high school where she taught catechism to young pupils enrolled.

In 2000, as a student at the National Polytechnic Institute - INPHB - of Yamoussoukro, in Ivory Coast, she took part with the Founder ACKAH Bilé Daniel, in her capacity as Head of the 1st promotion of the Ministry, in the creation of the MICI (*Ministry of Intercession for Ivory Coast with a 500 membership strength on several continents*). She retains this position since 2012 and till date, she is a member of the council of elders of the MICI.

In 2008, she received a vision from the Lord for women and children while finishing her training in France and created the "School for Life" mission.

She then founded KOEUR de Miel Organisation, an event company specialized in charity and social work through its KOEUR EN OR Foundation, contributing benevolently to the building of several ministries to which the organization is affiliated.

In 2010, she participates with Moderator Epherlin KOFFI, as Deputy Leader in the creation of CENACLE Organization, which will become the Missionary Apostolate of CENACLE, based in several parishes in Abidjan and the West African Sub-region.

In the same year, she began courses in Theology for Laity at the UCAO (Catholic University of West Africa), and will graduate 3 years later.

During all these years, she took part in evangelism missions, broadcasts on Christian radio stations and spiritual retreats, as minister, organizer or gospel singer.

Returning to France in 2013, she created the French section of the MICI, with the mission of interceding for Ivory Coast and France.

In 2016, she founded the International Apostolate Generation Deborah - AIGD, present in Europe and Africa.

By training, Mimyelle is an Actuary (graduate in Ivory Coast), Strategist in Economic Intelligence and Expert in Risk Management (graduate in France).

Since 2016, she has been tirelessly contributing her quota to Christian Literature, authoring accessible and seasoned books for the spiritual edification of GOD's children.

Some Actions of KOEUR de Miel organisation

-

"A DROP OF WATER TO TRANSFORM LIVES."

Among all the actions carried out by KOEUR de Miel Organization, we will talk about the concept and the caravan called :

"A drop of water to transform lives" organized in 2012 - 2013 (post-crisis period) in Côte d'Ivoire.

This caravan took place in 3 stages:

- Christmas tree in Duekoué and ZEO
- Christmas Tree in Man
- Luncheon donation at Bingerville Psychiatric Hospital.

In total, at the end of this caravan of love and charity, about 500 children in Man and Zéo were given toys for Christmas 2012 and 55 patients from the psychiatric hospital in Bingerville were provided with kits. The social service of the psychiatric hospital has estimated that the medicines donated could be used to cater for the needs of 20 other patients.

I. <u>Christmas Tree in DUEKOUE and Zeo Parish</u>

The Cassava producing district is one of the most underprivileged areas of the city of DUEKOUE (Central Côte d'Ivoire). The primary school "Ste Thérèse artisanale" was set up in 2009, following a serious accident in which two children aged 7 and 8 were run over by a motorist on their way to school, about 3 km from their village. The first child died on the spot, while the second was paralyzed for life. Unfortunately, this school, which was opened to the delight of the villagers, had no infrastructure. At the initiative of the director, classes were erected in bamboo, without roof - nothing safe from the weather.

At the time, the school had a staff of 150 students from CP1 to CM2, supervised by a group of 6 teachers.

Each student and teacher's child received a kit consisting of toys, food and clothing.

After Duékoué, we donated for the Christmas Tree organized by the Parish of Zéo.

II. Christmas tree at the Man NURSERY.

The Christmas tree in Man followed a previous mission of charitable actions (donations of food and clothing), carried out at the NGO "La Pépinière" in August 2012.

The NGO "la pépinière" was founded by the late Mrs. KOFFI (who *died in 2015*). Located in Man, an area of Côte d'Ivoire deeply affected by the war, the NGO "la pépinière" receives orphaned, abandoned or simply needy children who are taken care of, materially and intellectually. The reception center offers both an educational and vocational training (nursery, primary, sewing, hairdressing, carpentry and computer science), and a dispensary. In total, about 400 recipients were provided for, each student receiving numerous toys, food and clothing.

Some pictures

Arbre de Noël à l'ONG la pépinière de MAN

CENTRE DE FORMATION PROFESSIONNELLE
Sainte Rita

III. <u>Donations to Bingerville Psychiatric Hospital</u>

The psychiatric hospital of Bingerville is the only structure in Côte d'Ivoire able to receive psychiatric cases. Unfortunately, this hospital is very dilapidated and has many material needs.

In partnership with FEED ME and Glory Business, KOEUR de Miel Organisation and CENACLE Organisation organised on Saturday 05 January 2013, a day of donation to the social service of the said hospital, and to each of its interns. The ceremony started with a copious meal shared with the patients, the staff present and some children from the surrounding concessions. Then followed the IGWE evening (concept of worship evening, from CENACLE Organisation) with renowned Christian artists. It was clear that the patients had been waiting for such moment for a long time.

To top it all, the outreach culminated the night with the distribution of snacks and gifts to patients, which gracefully made available in part by generous donors, were distributed as follows:

1. Each resident received a "dignity" kit containing:

§   A sponge
§   A towel
§   A soap
§   A toothbrush
§   A toothpaste
§   Washing powder
§   A rubber plate
§   A rubber glass
§   A rubber spoon

2. The Bingerville Psychiatric Hospital social service received, for prospective residents:

Ø One carton of psychiatric medication, worth 200,000 FCFA
Ø Seals
Ø Mops
Ø Mats
Ø Clothing
Ø Soap, washing powder, bleach.

3. Finally, the social service staff received a carton of milk to encourage them in their work.

Some pictures

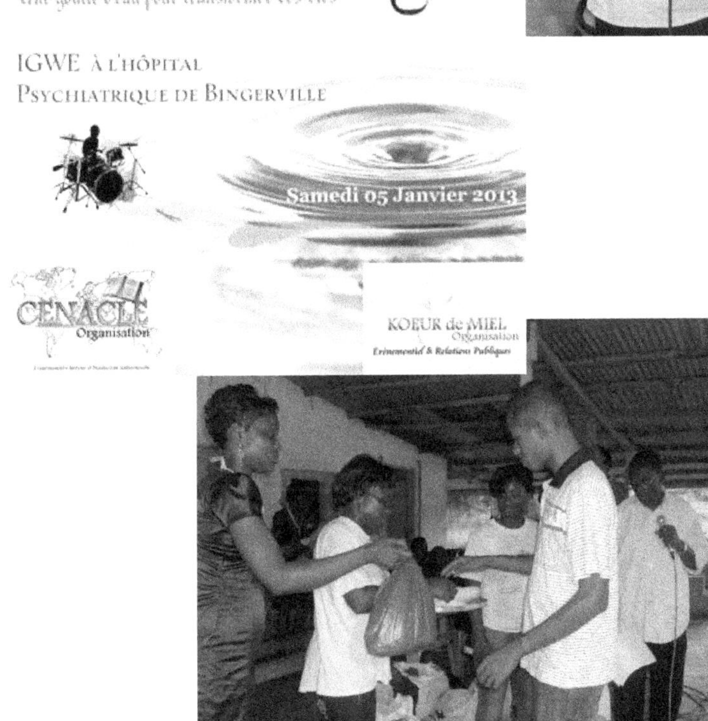

To contact us

KOEUR de MIEL Editions
An entity of the Lyketh & Co Group
6 rue d'Armaillé 75017 Paris
www.lyketh.fr

editions@lyketh.fr
mimyellek@gmail.com

France: + 337 82 32 68 29

USA: + 1 (571) 575-5428

Table of Contents

Printed in France